John Smith

The Hermit of Erving Castle,

Erving, Mass

John Smith

The Hermit of Erving Castle,
Erving, Mass

ISBN/EAN: 9783744794114

Printed in Europe, USA, Canada, Australia, Japan

Cover: Foto ©ninafisch / pixelio.de

More available books at **www.hansebooks.com**

THE HERMIT

OF

Erving Castle,

ERVING, MASS.

ERVING.

PUBLISHED FOR THE BENEFIT OF THE HERMIT.

1871.

In giving this book to the Public, as I do by request, I feel called upon to express my thanks to those who have so kindly assisted me in my undertaking.

Feeling grateful to the Public for former kindnesses,

I am, very respectfully,

JOHN, THE HERMIT.

ERVING CASTLE,
Erving, Mass., Sept., 1871.

THE HERMIT.

BY EDGAR L. MORSE.

In the bold and boastful Bay State,
   Just north-west of Erving town,
On the rocky pine clad hill side,
   Is a spot of such renown,

That upon the barren faces,
   Of the ridge that heavenward tends,
Excellently carved or painted,
   Are the names of many men.

Men from villas in the valleys,
   From the hamlets and the hills,
Men of low degree, and those who
   High positions nobly fill.

What can tempt this visitation ?
   What attract the eager throng ?
Patiently peruse this poem,
   And you'll ascertain ere long.

At the foot of this stupendous
   Ridge of boulders, which, to pave
Nature marvellously ventured,
   Is a roomy, gloomy cave.

It is evening,—I will enter,
   Since the throng has homeward sped,
In a nich within the cavern,
   Flash the flames with faggots fed.

Opposite, with blankets tattered,
   Soiled, forbidding to the touch,
Ricketty with age, devoid of
   Comliness, there stands a couch.

Surely, these are indications
   Of some human being's home,
You exclaim! You've spoken truly,
   'Tis the Hermit's, sad and lone.

And I slightly shudder, as he,
   At this instant with a smile,
Hastes to greet me,—but recover,
   Seeing naught portending guile.

Clothed in garments, ragged, thread-bare,
   Dingy; else but patches naught;
Face as bearded as a lion's,
   Yet with no such fierceness fraught.

Such was his appearance. Giving
   Me a seat, he then withdrew
To the corner where the flickering
   Flames their radience o'er him threw.

Then with loquacious glibness,
   Showed he those alloquial powers
Which have entertained so many,
   Many anxious minds for hours.

But his words were all unheeded,
   Little interest they bore,
For the study of his features
   Interested me far more.

How advertently I pondered
   On that visage. I could see
On that forehead sorrow's traces,
   Marks of deep anxiety.

There had care deep ploughed its furrows,
   Disappointment shed its gloom,
And his looks lacked that contentment
   Which affords to them their bloom.

Then I queried, why he'd chosen
   This abode so sad and drear,
Far away from human dwelling,
   Why retirement seemed so dear?

Why he loved to hear the evening
   Breeze go moaning through the trees,
Through the hemlock, pine and maples,
   Chanting mournful elegies?

Why the roaring of the tempest
   Did not drive him from his home,
As it sweeps about the barriers,
   Round about this rocky dome?

Why? unless these scenes so lonely,
   Were the symbols of his soul;
Emblematic of those feelings,
   Which for ever scorn control.

Curiosity and pity
   Soon induced me to inquire,
What wrecked this fallen being?
   His reply brought sadness dire.

'Twas the same, the same old story
   Oft repeated, told again,—
Broken-hearted by affection
   Not returned, of hope the bane.

DARTMOUTH COLLEGE, Hanover, N. H.

THE HERMIT OF ERVING CASTLE.

THE FIRST YEARS.

I, John the Hermit, landed on the shores of America, in May of the year 1866. I am a native of Perthshire, Scotland. As my father was a soldier, I know little about my birth. My mother died when I was a child, so I can tell little of my parentage. My grandmother took charge of me till she died, then I was sent to a government school till I was about 13 years of age. When my grandmother died she left me in charge of an old woman, called Tibby Scugle, This woman had been a lodger in the house with her several years. My mother was lady's maid to lady McDonald, for 15 years, before she married the soldier. It was at Greasley Abbey where they were married, it was at the same she died. On her death bed old Tib promised to take charge of me, and she did so with a hard struggle, for she had to earn her bread by washing. She might have been a great deal better off if she had not fell a victim to the dram glass, but with all her faults she never forsook the orphan boy. I remember my grandmother often was angry at her, and used to say when she saw her come at night, with her apron full of bits of soap, candle, lumps of beef and many other things, "Tibby my woman where did you get all this?" she would reply, "It is only my perquisites, and little enough, I trow."

On the other side of the street was the "Beggars' Opera," which is a large lodging house for all kinds of impostors, from the gentleman beggar to the dandy thief. The house was a great amusement to me, for through the window I could see all their schemes of fraud carried on.

This house was a regular resort for Tib. If ever so tired she never could go to bed without going over the way, as she used to call it, and very often it was difficult to get home again sober. I used to see her deep in conversation with an old man who went by the name of the "dandy matchman." This old man knew the country far and wide. If a robbery was to be done he was almost sure to be at the head of it. One Saturday afternoon, I was surprised to see Tibby seated by the fire, in our house, holding a deep conversation with my grandmother, and "the dandy matchman." "Well, marm, this gentleman says he knows Mr. Allen well," and pointing to me says, in a whisper to the scamp, "Is he any way like him?" "Just the image, from the crown of his head to the sole of his foot," he replied.

I was at a loss to know what a Mr. Allen had to do with me. My mother's name was Allen before she married my father, but as I had never seen any relative besides I have mentioned, I was in no hurry to get any acquaintance.

"Law, see marm," says Tibby to my grandmother, "he is very rich, and might make a gentleman of the lad."

My grandmother, in one of her foolish moments, had told Tibby of my uncle, a son of hers, who was in good circumstances, he had left her in a quarrel, a long time before I was born, she had never heard of his whereabouts since, and she was too proud to inquire, till Tibby bethought herself of the dandy matchman. "So you say it will take a week to travel there?" she says to the man. "O, yes,

marm, for it is beyont Aberdeen, and the lad is but a strip-
ling, and marm you cannot go along without a few shillings
in your pocket, marm, to appear respectable, for I do as-
sure you, marm, Mr. Allen is a gentleman."

Tibby handed the broken glass to the man, which he
took with a bow, putting it to his mouth, he replied, "ye es
do always keep the good stuff, marm," and returning the
glass, took his leave.

As soon as he was gone, turning to my grandmother,
Tibby said, "I have got a £5 note from her ladyship, to buy
him some clothes. It was a mean sum to give, but it will
help us on the road. At any rate, his clothes will have to
do. If I can but get the right side of the gentleman; he is
able to get plenty clothes for him."

So Monday was set for our tramp for Aberdeen. On
Sunday Tibby was so taken up with the old dandy matchman, and the broken glass and bottle, that I began to think
there would be little of the money left for the road.

At last Monday morning came, and me with a bundle of
clothes, or rags rather, across my shoulders, with my friend
Tibby, took the road.

My grandmother had her doubts about my reception, but
Tib, with a club in her hand, and the old glass and bottle
in her pocket, took the road. Every now and then, she must
give me a little information of this rich uncle of mine, and
taking another drop from the bottle, would start off again,
and every body she met, she would inquire if we was on
the right road to Aberdeen. Some thought she was mad,
others said she had stolen me, and was on the road to
sell me to the doctors. But Tib, undaunted, pushed on. She
took lodgings at the farm houses, to save expenses, she said,
but I found out she wished to replenish the bottle rather.

After a week, tramping, we came in sight of Aberdeen. Tibby began to brush me up a bit. And washing herself at the brook, by the way side, bethought herself, it was too late to reach the house of Mr. Allen that night. It would be better to put up at a tavern, so turning down a street, we came in sight of "The Horse and Jockey." Catching me by the hand, she marched up to the landlady, and asked for lodgings, which were granted. So taking a seat by the fire, the landlady asked, "if we wished for supper." Tib said "as she was very tired, she would prefer a glass of whiskey, till the supper was ready." What with the fire and whiskey together, I thought she would never have done asking about this great Mr. Allen, the rich uncle of mine.

Early on the following morning she rose, and putting on her best clothes, which were but rags, and taking me by the hand, she started off.

But to my dying day, I shall never forget the reception we got at my rich uncle's.

When we came to the house, although I was a lad of 9 years of age, I was at a loss to find my way to the door, for in front was a garden, or rather a forest of thistles and nettles; the gate was nailed up, with a board, and letters written thereon, "round the corner to the kitchen door, but beware of the dogs." I thought we were far enough, so turning to Tibby, I asked her what she thought of the rich uncle now?

" I troth and sure I am not gone to come so far and not to see him indade." So pushing open a gate of a pen of cattle, she was marching her way towards the door of the house, when all of a moment a man with whip in hand came up, and giving Tib. a strike with it, demanded, " what we vagrants was doing among his cattle?"

" Vagrants ?" replied Tib, and throwing off her old red
cloak, she, with club in hand asked him what he meant by
insulting a dacent woman ? who had come, more than a hundred miles, to bring his sister's son to him."

With this a tall woman came to the door, and looking at
me, from head to foot, declared " we was nothing but impos-
ters, for" she said "there was not a drop of the Allen's
blood in me." She insisted upon her brother's giving Tibby
a sound good whipping, and sending her, and her brat away,
for so she called me.

Tibby was so enraged at the woman's insolence, that without any further ceremony, she made a bold dash at the man
with her club, he with his whip, so I clung to Tib's apron,
shouting out ten thousand murders, and to make matters
worse, the dog came to be third man. At last the town con-
stable, arrived on the spot, and siezing Tib, with one hand,
and me, with the other, marched us off to the stocks, where
we both got our feet locked up for four hours, and to stand
all the insults from the rabble of the town ; for some bat-
tered us with mud and stones.

At last we were marched out of town as vagrants.

Tib. had spent all the money, in the expectation of finding
a fresh supply at my rich uncle's, so we had to beg our way
home.

The trip fairly cured poor Tib, from going across the
way, for to get news from " The Dandy Matchman." And
I gave up all hopes of ever becoming my rich uncle's heir.

THE WANDERINGS.

When the school days were over, I took a notion to become a packman, or a peddler as they are called in this country. Lady McDonald gave me a handsome box for my

jewelry and £5 in money to start with. I next stole away
to my father, who was now married again. My grandmother was at variance with him. My mother had married him against her will, and since her death, my grandmother had forbidden me to go to see him. Before I
reached the house, he saw me at a distance, and ran to meet
me. His wife also treated me kindly, for she gave me £10
out of her own pocket, and I believe she would have been
a good step-mother to me, had it not been for my grand
mother.

I next bought my goods and started out for the low country. I did very well, for a beginner and a mere boy, for
I was only 15 years of age.

As the winter came on, I did not like it as well, and on
coming back for Glasgow again, I met an old friend who
said he had engaged for the winter at the " Grand Imperial
Turkish Tent," and that they wanted several others also. I
went with him, for I had a good taste for the stage. So I
engaged myself for the season, to commence the following
week, with the grand performance of " The Enchanted Castle on the Plains of Bavaria."

I became a good actor and at the end of the season had
saved £20.

LOVE'S FATAL STORM.

As soon as the Spring came in, I thought I had best be
up and doing. I did not fancy to be always polishing knives
and rings, so I thought it best to try dry goods, as the ladies
are in general the best buyers; and to take to "The Highlands," instead of the "Lowlands," as the people there are
thought to be the kindest.

So I started for Inverness. I was in a strange part of the

country, and in crossing the Grampians, I lost myself in the mountains; for some times the fog rises and for hours you cannot see a yard before you. The night came on, I still kept moving about; at midnight it was very chilly, but I thought if I lay down, I should never rise again, so I wandered about. At last the day began to dawn. I got up on a piece of high rock, to see if any houses could be seen, for I was getting quite exhausted, I thought that at a distance I could perceive one, so I made my way towards it. As I came in sight of the house, the smoke began to rise from the kitchen chimney. I did not know how to show myself, in such a figure, for one of my trowsers legs was nearly torn off with falling amongst the bushes. But what made it worse, it was Sunday. I reached the door, but it was all I could do, I had no power to rap, for down I fell. The door was opened by an old woman who gave a loud scream, and ran away. I was struggling to reach the fire, when a young woman entered in her morning gown. I heard her say, "Run and wake up my father, but let's shift him from the fire first as I have heard them say it is fatal for a sudden heat, after starvation."

They laid a mattress on the floor and me thereon, the old woman went to raise the house. While she was away, the other began to get my wet clothes off. The house was soon all in a stir, some said give him some whiskey to drink, others cried for warm milk, but I do not know what they gave me, for I soon fell into a deep sleep, which lasted so long that they thought that I was never going to wake up again. Towards evening I opened my eyes, and began to show some signs of life. I began to wonder how I got there, for I had no recollection of what had passed. The young woman sat near me, reading a book, she let it fall and called for her father, who came in haste and said "Betsey, my child get him some tea now, for he is out of danger." She soon had it ready and came with it to the place where I was lying. "Betsey, my lass," cried her father, "you are an angel; it was you that watched the last breath from your poor mother depart; it was you that heard her last prayer, while the salt tears rolled down my cheek; I tell thee to watch the lad, and the angels bless thee, my darling!"

Betsey did as her father had told her, and I could not help looking at the lovely Betsey, till she stole my heart away. For several days I was not able to walk without help, she scarcely ever left me, till I was able to move about. As soon as I got better, I said I must take my leave, as all my goods were booked for Inverness, and no doubt would be lost. As the words fell upon her ear, her cheek grew pale. I felt I cannot tell how; was it love? how could it be? and she a lady? for her father was very rich and she his only daughter; it was a mountain home and Betsey had seen but little of the world then. What a pity it was, that I should have wrung her loving heart in speechless sorrow.

THE BROKEN RING.

The morning came, so I said I must take me leave. Betsey and her youngest brother, a youth about my own age, were at the door with their own team, to take me safe out of the mountains. In a suit of this youth's clothes they dressed me, for my own were so torn that I could not wear them.

As we reached the hotel where the stage coach was to take me on, she said—"Shall we never meet again?"

My heart beat, and my tongue was speechless. I took her hand, and pressed it to my lips. She said "Good by till we meet again." I got into the coach; as it started, I turned to look at the lovely maiden. She was stepping into the carriage to depart, her eye caught mine, and with a smile we parted, with a promise soon to meet again. She was in deep mourning at the time for her mother, who had died but a few weeks before; her dress was rich, but plain, not a ruffle was to be seen as the black crape veil fell over her shoulders; on her head she had no waterfall, but her rich auburn hair was done up in plain neat braids; like an angel's form she left me, but her phantom followed me; in my dreams I saw her, by day my thoughts were all on Betsey, and now I fancy I see her as plain as the night. We broke the ring in two. As soon as I reached Inverness and found my goods right. I took up lodgings with an old woman in Ness street. It was not quite the place I liked, but as I did not intend to remain longer than to dispose of my goods, I put up with it.

In a few days there came a letter from Betsey, requesting me to come to the "Elms," before I returned to Glasgow, The farm took its name. owing to large elm trees, that formed the avenues in front of the house. It was beneath these trees she gave me the ring, some twelve months after, as I was leaving her to go to Glasgow and to London for the winter.

THE VOW.

Here is a token of true love, let us break it in two, here's half my heart and half my ring to shew my love for you.

The moon shed her midnight gleams amongst the branches, as we retired from the place so sacred.

On the following morning I left the Elms, with Betsey's promise to follow me, as soon as I could get a suitable lodging place for her.

While on the stage at Glasgow, I had become acquainted with a charming young actress, Miss Fannie Tysdal, she had a brother named Robert, one of the leading actors of the day. I was Fanny's comrade on the stage, and if any love affair was to be acted, it always fell to our share. It was upon her account I was going to London, for she had taken an engagement in one of the theatres there, and to make a better show of it, had put my name on the bills as Mr. Robert Tysdal.

We were to commence with the beautiful love tragedy of "The Young Tyrole" or "The Italian Shepherdess." It is one of the finest love pieces that ever came on the stage.

A few days brought Betsey to London. I had got the liberty of a seat unoccupied, near the Duchess of B——, that she might have a full view of the tragedy.

In the full dress of a Tyrole youth, I handed her into the pew, and hasted to the stage, for the curtain was already drawn, and Fanny already, as the Italian Shepherdess on the plain where I was to meet her. I had given Betsey a bill of performance, forgetting, as I did so, that I had a false name on it. As soon as she saw the name, it was too much for her, she at once took me for an imposter, and when she saw me and Fanny playing the part so well together, she at once despised me in her heart. As soon as my part was finished I went into the side room to change my dress, to be able to take Betty to her lodgings; but she was gone; I followed after but it was of no use, she told me to be gone for an imposter as I was.

The next day she set off for the Elms. I wrote to her father and told him all about it. He answered my letter and said he would try all he could to convince her how it happened; but it was of no use; poor girl, she had never seen

much of the world then, being brought up in the mountains.
I think Fanny was in love with me, for she often said she
would marry me if I would say yes. I'm sure I loved Fanny, but Betty far more, for Betty was my first love.

Our acting turned out to be a good job for the company,
for the managers published it in every paper, and the theatre
was crowded every night, more to see Fanny and myself who
was the unfortunate lovers inste ad of the Young Tyrole.

THE COLLIERS' STRIKE IN 1844-5.

My location at this time, in the city of Glasgow, was not
in a very fashionable street, being on the lower part of the
old town.

All the wealthy merchants had moved up into what was
called the "New City;" thus the houses where the rich
once lived had become the houses of the poor.

But the house where I was lodging had never been the
abode of the rich, only when they were brought there to be
burned at the stake.

On one side of the court were three blocks of stone where
the martyrs were chained and burned. In the center of the
court stands the house, with massive walls of stone 9 feet
thick. An archway extends through the center of the honse,
large enough to admit the passage of carriages.

In the cellar are stone benches which were used as beds
for the poor victims.

It was a hard time for the poor ; coal was not to be had ; the
country was in arms ; soldiers were marching in all directions. Smith O'Brien had moved all Ireland, as well as
part of England. Scotland was impatient to join the fracas.
The king of France had fled, and landed at Holyrood palace
where the queen had given him shelter.

Public places were closed, and the streets blockaded to keep out the mob.

I had been up all night, finishing some fancy mats for the Mirthley Castle, and just as the sun was lighting up the noisy streets, my old landlady opened the door and in mournful tone said, "John I want you to take breakfast with me this morning; it is just three years since my husband died and I do not like to be alone." I consented, and, as we were partaking her bounties, the street criers were shouting in all tones, and voices; here comes an old Jew, shouting out "old clothes."

"What is that, is it coal, John?" said the old woman, "that is all the coal I have," she continued, " it was not so when Tom was alive, Lord bless his soul," and crossing herself, she prayed for the Lord to send her relief, and I know not how long she would have continued, had I not interrupted her by saying, "Mrs. Cordon, there is a rap at the street door, shall I answer it?"

"No," she said, "it is only that drunken grany again," and catching up the broom, off she started towards the door.

I was expecting to see her return with a "drunken jade," as she called her, but what was my surprise on hearing her say, "your feet must be cold laddie, I have a pair of old shoes, and John will give you a pair of hose, won't you John?" and she led into the room a boy, with a few bundles of sticks under his arms; he had neither shoes or stockings, although the ground was white with snow.

"My lad," said I, "sit down and I will see what can be done for you." He drank a cup of tea that the landlady had placed before him, but refused to eat; " are you not hungry? eat if you can, you are welcome to my part; put those sticks on the fire, I will pay for them." "Thank you,

sir," he said. "Where do you live ? is your father alive ?"
"My father is in heaven where I shall soon meet him."
"Your mother, where is she ?" at that name he turned deathly
pale, and gave a slight groan ; my conscience smote me, I
had done wrong to wound so young a heart.

My sympathy was kindled for the little fellow, and turning
around towards the landlady, said, "have you not a bed
on which your own little boy died ? let this one have it and
I will meet all the expenses. As soon as the lad had re-
vived, I said, "if you will stay with me, I will be your
father, until you meet your other father in heaven." The
tears started down the little boy's cheeks, and catching
my hand, he said, " you are very kind, but God will not let
me trouble you long ; my earthly wants are nearly over ; in
heaven there is no suffering, for Jesus says, he will feed all
without money and without price."

I felt ashamed that one so young should teach me such
lessons of trust and love toward the blessed Savior. By this
time the landlady had prepared a warm bath, and as I was
undressing him, I discovered his back and limbs were black
and swollen, caused by recent beatings. Upon my question-
ing him, he said, "it was done with a man who lived
with his mother," he said his mother was not what she used
to be, but was drunk all the time, and lived with this wicked
man."

As soon as he was asleep, I searched his clothes and found
a silk purse, which contained four shillings, two and one half
pence ; on one side of the purse were these words, "Sometimes think of me." I also found a hymn book and a small
brush, which the laddie gave me when he died shortly after,
and I have them now, at the Hermitage, among my few
treasured things.

The laddie still being quiet, I left him in the landlady's charge, and then started for some new clothes. The whole city was in an uproar; the riot act had been read, and the soldiers had had orders to clear the streets.

I went through Throne Gate, and reached High street. I saw a large crowd flying in all directions. To go on was not to be thought of; therefore I turned into old Venell street, which was more peaceful.

Here I saw an old man struggling for life, his face was clotted with blood, and his clothes were torn to rags; in a feeble voice he asked for help; but just at this time, an old woman came up with her dress converted into a basket, which was filled with bits of cheese, candles, coal and old iron, which she had picked up in the streets. "Help?" she said, " I know that voice, rascal, find help you gave me; when my poor husband died, you turned me and my five little children into the streets, for only six months rent, and then while wandering about, sleeping sometimes on their father's grave, my little darling froze in its mother's arms; bleed on 'till the last drop of blood shall have flown from thy veins; stay thy hand grievous death, and let him die a thousand deaths in one." At this she moved on, muttering horrid curses upon the head of McEagin. The mob had broken into his store, and, finding him hid in a large box, dragged him out by the hair of his head, and trampled him under their feet.

At last I arrived at the Jews' quarters. I had not gone far before I was saluted, and asked if I wished to trade? "I will sell you a suit of clothes very cheap, please walk in." I stepped into the room which was very dark, the windows being boarded, but soon the gas was lighted, and I purchased a suit of clothes for £3, and started for home. The soldiers had cleared the streets, but I received a blow from a brick that was thrown from the top of a house by a rebel, otherwise I arrived safely home.

The morning had been stormy and the waves of the sea were rolling mountains high.

As I opened the door of the house, I perceived the landlady upon her knees, pleading with the advocate above, for a disobedient son, whom the father had put away some years before his death, and she had never heard of him since, and like Jacob, she was going down to the grave and weeping because he was not. As I listened to her from the outside of the closet, these words fell upon my ear : "Almighty Father, thou that swayest the universe as if it were nothing, say to these proud waves, be still, for the sake of my poor wanderer ; Lord, it is enough, upon me let thy anger fall, only restore my only son. His father has crossed the river, and landed safe on the other side. His brother, my little darling has tuned his harp with the throng above ; and I am lingering on the banks till these few sands of time drop out, and shall one which thou hast given me be wanting? O heavenly Father, spare his life till he has made his peace with Thee. This night let another name be enrolled in thy everlasting record book, and thine shall be the glory forever."

As soon as the old lady had finished her prayer, I resumed work on the mats.

The boy was still asleep and seemed very much wearied. I told the old lady that I hoped he'd not die, for he would be a great comfort to me in my old age.

Soon, however, the boy awoke, and looking around, inquired for his clothes. "I have burned them," I said "but here are some new ones for you, I saved all that was found in your pockets and here they are."

He arose and seemed to be refreshed, but his cough told plainly that his earthly career was nearly over. I tried to cheer him, and as he was fond of music, I commenced to sing, and as I was singing, "There is a fountain filled with blood," &c., he tried to join me, but his breath failed him. When I had finished, he asked me, "if I had ever been washed in that fountain?" Those words went like daggers to my heart; I could not speak and he continued, " I know that fountain is open for all, for Jesus died that we might live." Yes, indeed, the lad spoke truly, for Christ Jesus himself, says, "Whosoever will may come," and dear friends, one and all, he says, " Now is the accepted time."

The next morning I received a letter from Lady McDonald, asking me to come and spend a few weeks with her, till the rebels were put down, and enclosed with the letter was £5 to defray expenses.

I wrote immediately and told her just how I was situated, and in a few days, a hamper, loaded with provisions and two blankets, arrived for the boy from Lady McDonald. The boy being no better, I sent for Dr. Duff, who, after examining him, said he had not many days to live. When the boy heard this, he said he wished to see his mother and two sisters who were living in Edinburgh. The boy's bruises were very bad, and the Dr. wished me to go with him and find the inhuman monster and have him arrested.

The next morning we started on the seven o'clock train, and reached the capital at nine o'clock.

We took a cab and requested the driver to leave us at the Horse Wind, near the New Gate. The man looked at us and said he was afraid to go there again, as the last time he was there he came near being killed, and his horse and cab were badly damaged.

We calmed his fears, and started off through the grass marked into a narrow street, where the old dirty houses of five or six stories, together with the old rubbish of all kinds and descriptions lying around, and the squallid set of people plainly told of " Poverty, hunger and dirt."

Soon the driver stopped and pointed up to a narrow alley and said, "Gents, that is the house," we paid him, and off he started at full speed, as if he was afraid to stay, and judging from appearances, I should not blame him for it was really the worst place I ever visited, and I have never seen the like since.

After some difficulty we reached the house, judging from the boy's descriptions. After we had rapped several times, the door was opened. I started back, for before me stood a being, whether male or female it was hard to say. An old red shawl and ragged petticoat comprised the clothing of this person, but judging from the long matted hair, which very much resembled a cow's tail, we concluded it was a woman.

She stared at us like a mad tigress, and when I asked if the master of the house was in, she said, " And what may you want of Master Jazman ?" " I wish to see him," I re-plied, " and that as soon as possible, for we wish to return by the six o'clock train."

At this she started down a narrow passage and said, " out with the gas, lads, at the door are two bobbies* from Glas-gow." Hold your blathering tongue," cried a voice from within, " they are neither bobbies nor policemen, for they'd never stop to rap, the house would have been searched, and we handcuffed and off to the stone jug long before this, if they had been.

* Disguised Policemen.

A young man now came up the passage with one eye swollen, and the other bandaged, and a large cut across his face. After taking a look at us, he returned apparently satisfied; the old woman came back rubbing her face with a dish cloth, and looking more like the evil one than ever; she went to the foot of a large stone stairway and called several times, at length a feeble voice replied, "What is it Sue?" "Here are two strangers waiting for you." "Tell them I am engaged," he said. "They are from Glasgow and wish very much to see you." "Well I'll try and come down, but Sue, show them up here, my gout is so bad." Then she said, "This way if you must see the old crone, but you'll not get much out of him, I guess, he is not the man to inform on his lodgers, they pay too well for that."

On reaching the head of the stairs, we were lead across a large hall, and ushered into the presence of the Jazman.

The old man was sitting by the fire, with his feet resting on a soft cushion, he was badly afflicted with the gout.

"Walk in and shut the door," he said. We did so, and were soon engaged in the object of our visit.

The Dr. commenced by telling him we had come to inquire concerning a poor boy who had been abused in his house, and to see his mother, who, we understood was lodging there. The old man said, "that the lodgers were often engaged in fighting, but he left all those things to Sue. What is the boy's name? "Tyran," replied the Dr. "Tyran? Tyran, did you say?" he eagerly asked, and clasping his hands, the tears flowing down his cheeks, said, "Lord have mercy on his wicked soul. Did you not know that the woman had killed herself and child? Dads was a cruel woman and would abuse herself and her children to a most shameful and wicked extent; and as the shades of last night's sun-set were falling over the city, she stole away to the outskirts of the town, and in a dark lane, cut her poor darling's throat with a sharp razor, and then with the same instrument put an end to her own existence.

We asked the old man a few more questions, but he could tell us little concerning the man.

He said he had rented his garret for two years to the woman, and she had been very faithful in paying her weekly half-crown.

We then took our leave of the landlord; on our way down stairs, we saw two young men running from the house, closely followed by Sue with a poker in her hand, just then she said, "you had better not come back here till you bring some money, burning my coal at two shillings per hundred, and the gas"—here my attention being so taken up with the old woman, I stumbled and fell head long over the heads of two young women, who were sitting on the stairs; I immediately asked their pardon, but they would hear nothing of pardon, one said she wished I'd broke my neck; the other "wondered if Glasgow folks had nothing to do, but to run after an old fool of a woman; if she was tired of life, it was a good plan to get rid of herself."

"Poor woman," said the Dr. "I pity your ignorance."— "I ask no pity at your hands;—no pity I give, no pity I crave; as I have made my bed so let me lie;" then turning to the others, she continued, "you may think me mad, you may think me crazy; I am neither;" striking her breast with her hands, she said, "within this breast once breathed a woman's heart, and in that heart a woman's love, but that love has been abused, my spirit is broken, my blood freezes in their veins.; I was deluded from my father's house, by a young man, who left me in this den of infamy, my poor old mother died of grief for her only child, my father weeping still prays for the return of his lost daughter. I have hardened my heart and drowned my griefs in the cursed cup. But, oh ! hardened as I am, I still sometimes think of my former home, and oh ! I sigh for one hour's peace, such as I used to have in my father's house."

" Poor girl," said I, " where does your father live ? I will go and see him, and do anything to restore you to his loving embrace."

" My father lives on the farm of Gowenbray." " What, is his name James Lawrence ?" cried the Dr., " and is this my old friend,—the lovely Sally ?—my joy will be complete if I can return you safe to your father's arms. I saw your mother when she breathed her last. I heard her last words, as she breathed a prayer for you. Her spirit is still pleading at the throne of grace for your redemption. Stay no longer in this place of hell, go with us and we will place you safe in your father's house. Let there be joy in heaven this night over one strayed sheep that has returned to the shepherd's fold."

" I will arise and go to my father, I will no longer feed upon the husks of wickedness." At this her companion burst into tears and said, " Sally, do not leave me here, we have been friends for several years. O, don't leave me." The old woman let her poker fall as though a thunderbolt had struck her, and turning to Sally, she said, " What is the matter, I never heard you talk like this before ?" But the Dr. interrupted her by saying, "We must be going." At this, Sally's companion wept bitterly and said she must not leave her. "I will not," said Sally, "you have shared my sorrow, you shall share my joy. In my father's house there is room, and he will be your father too."

We then took leave of the old woman. The Dr. wished to be present at the inquest to be held over the dead bodies, so at his request I returned with the girls to his house.

The Dr.'s wife, who was a very kind woman, wished to see the boy, so leaving the girls there, I went with her to my lodgings. When we entered the court, we saw a coach and six standing at the door, which I recognized as that of Lady Fitz Gerald of Drummond Castle.

This lady was very rich, and spent a great share of her income in relieving the poor, and a much better way than to be making a great display to satisfy vanity.

In all large cities, my friends, and even in some of the small towns, are many who, when night comes, have no where to lay their heads. I am poor, but when I cast in my mite to help any sufferer, I feel as if God would restore it ten fold. " Cast thy bread upon the waters, for thou shalt find it after many days." Eccl. xi. 1.

The Dr. returned in the afternoon, and after examining the boy, said he could live but a few days.

The Sheriff ordered the arrest of the man and offered £20 to any one who would cause his apprehension.

The mother's tragedy had caused great excitement, and such crowds flocked to the house, that a guard had to be stationed before the door to prevent accidents.

The bodies of the mother and the child were taken to the " White Hart," the ladies of St. Mary's convent taking the charge of them there.

The mother was laid out on the left side of the room, as she was a murderess, and the child on the right side, robed in white satin, with a wreath of white flowers twined about her head; she looked more like an angel than a murdered child.

A plate was placed on either side to receive subscriptions, which was soon filled. Such a murder had never happened in Scotland before.

Saturday the bodies were carried to the convent; the little child was placed at the foot of the altar to be dedicated to the Virgin. Sunday they were buried. After the procession left the Convent, they marched to north bridge, where they separated, and the ladies bearing the infant's coffin passed through, then the mother's coffin and the crowd fell in, to the number of five thousand, and marched to the grave. After the coffins were lowered to their narrow resting place, the Dr. stepped forward and said, "The scene is not ended, the tragedy is not finished, in a few days another poor sufferer, the only son of this poor woman, will close his life of suffering, caused by this same cruel monster, who is the real murderer of this woman and child; his earthly wants are nearly over, soon his soul will wing its flight to join his mother in the arms of Jesus."

The Captain of the police said that everything should be done that could be to secure this monster of wickedness.

Lady Fitz Gerald had kindly cared for the boy, while I was at the funeral, which being over I returned to him.

The Countess Selkirk and the S. S. children came soon after; the boy smiled and asked them if they had come to see him pass over to Jordan, to Canaan's happy shore.

He asked if some one would pray, and a noble looking youth stepped forward and taking his hand, sent up a petition that might make many a minister blush in silence. He said that that night there would be a great banquet in heaven; the King of kings was seated on his throne of love; angels with their crowns laid at the feet of Jesus, were waiting to receive the new born heir into the kingdom of heaven.

As soon as he had finished, the countess set her harp to
the beautiful tune of Auburn, and the children joined with
their clear voices with the words :—

> " Come let us join our cheerful songs,
> With angels round the throne, &c."

While they were singing he fell into a sweet sleep, and
the countess laid aside her harp.

He lingered along until the next night, when he opened
his eyes, and looking towards heaven said,—" Jesus, come."
I started and caught his hand, but all was over ; his spirit
had departed, and we imagined we could hear from the por-
tals of the sky a sweet voice saying, " Another pearl of love
set in the Redeemer's crown."

His death was published in all the city papers, and I received several letters containing money to defray expenses.
Sabbath was appointed for his funeral. At an early hour, a
procession was formed of nearly forty carriages, including
Lady Fitz Gerald and the Countess Selkirk. The carriage
containing the corpse was trimmed with white flowers and a
white velvet banner with a painting in the center represent-
ing the angels winging their flight through thick clouds to
receive his pure spirit into the realms of happiness.

On our way we met a large procession, bearing several
banners, on one of which were the words :—" No drunkard
can enter the kingdom of heaven."

As we halted a choir met us and commenced singing :—

> " Thou art worthy O Lord to receive, &c."

When they stopped singing a minister stepped forward
and said he wished to say a word, not for the dead but to
the living.

He commenced with these words, " When Jesus therefore saw her weeping, and the Jews also weeping which came with her, he groaned in the spirit and was troubled." John xi. 33. When he closed his excellent remarks scarcely a dry face could be seen in that assembly.

When we reached the new made graves of the mother and sister, we laid the poor boy to rest beside them. I was the last to leave his grave ; sad, indeed, was my heart, he seemed so pure and loving. O, if he could only come and lay my gray head beneath the dust, but that can never be. He was too rich a jewel to shine in this sinful world, and now he blooms in the beautiful garden of heaven. He told me he would look down from heaven and pray for me, and I sometimes think he does. It is a blessed thought at least, and one that would inspire every one to a noble life, if they would only trust and believe.

My friends, be not weary of well doing; God will bless you in this world, and in the world to come ye shall receive a crown of everlasting glory.

About three months after the death of my adopted son, I received a letter from Edinburg summoning me to appear at the court of justice on the next Monday. I did not like to appear in court, so I consulted the Dr. who had received a like summons, and we decided that it was best to go. The next Monday found us in the court room.

After the disposing of a few cases, we were informed that the next one was the one on which we had been summoned as witnesses. The door opened, and in was lead a mere dwarf of a man. Our astonishment was great ; we expected to see a giant almost.

A charge of brutality was read ; the prisoner listened until it concluded, then said, he had often been intoxicated, and had trouble with the woman, but the boy he knew nothing about, therefore he pleaded " Not guilty."

The witnesses were then examined; the first being the little boy's sister, a beautiful child of nine summers.

The judge asked her if she had ever seen that man before. She, trembling at the sight of him, said, " Yes, he has often kicked me, and I still carry the marks upon my person; I have seen him drag my brother by the hair of his head and kick him down stairs." After examining the other witnesses, the judge pronounced him guilty, and sentenced him to six years penal servitude.

When he was leaving the room, the woman, Sue, shouted out : " Cheer up, Jem, I will give you a hot supper before you go." The judge ordered her arrest, and sentenced her to six months servitude for contempt of court; thus she had plenty of time to prepare her hot supper.

About this time I received an invitation to accompany a man and his wife on a visit to her son, who was confined in a certain prison. That night we started for the prison and soon found ourselves within its walls. After being examined, we were introduced to the governor, who was a real gentleman, he was very kind to us; he said, he was sorry to inform us, that the prisoner's conduct had been such, that he had brought upon himself two severe punishments; he was now dying. My host said he was not the boy's father, and had no control over him. " But," said the governor, "you are to blame; when you married his mother, you should have taken care of the fatherless boy; but you turned him into the street, to starve or steal, and now he is dying in prison, and on your head rests the crime."

Then he lead us to the hospital, which was a large room with twenty-five beds on either side.

On the farther side lay the youth; as we approached his bed he did not notice us, but the mother stepping forward, said, " George, do you not know me ? " At this, he started and said, " Stand off ! you drove me to ruin, and are you come to torment me in my last moments ! hell is open for me, let me die." At this he uttered such a horrid list of oaths, that I was very sorry I had ever seen him.

After he had become composed, he said, " Do somebody pray for me ; O ! is there none to help me through this dark valley ? "

One person stepped up and said. " George, I'll try to introduce you to the throne of grace." We all joined with him in prayer, it has never been my fortune to hear elsewhere. While the tears were coursing down our cheeks, he was told to cling to Jesus ; if it was but the hem of his garments he touched, he would receive the sweet gift of forgiveness ; even as the dying thief, this man seemed to fall into the arms of Jesus.

" But friends," he said, " never do as I have ; Oh ! for a little while to show to others the mercy of Jesus." Yes, come to Jesus now and enjoy his goodness while here below and his glory hereafter.

The poor boy soon breathed his last, and the spirit returned to God who gave it.

This prison contained two thousand five hundred men, nine hundred women, and seven hundred boys.

Is there no way to prevent some of this misery ? Ah, yes ! when we shall have learned to be Christians, there will be no crime, or sorrow, but all will be peace and happiness.

After the rebels had been put down, and the affairs of State settled, the Countess asked me to spend a few weeks at the pavillion, but as I had a large lot of goods on hand, I thought it best to dispose of them as soon as possible; therefore I prepared for a trip among the railroad men, who were at work on the Caledonian railroad. It was in a wild country containing no houses within sixteen miles, except the mud houses of the workmen. The character of the men was such that few travelers dared go among them, but I was desirous of trying my luck, and off I started.

It was about fifty miles from Glasgow. I sent most of my goods on by coach to the nearest village. Taking a few fancy goods upon my back, I started on foot, intending to reach them the same day; it was late in the fall and the scenery was beautiful. I had traveled about ten miles when I came to a toll bridge across the Clyde.

Here I saw a woman, standing in the road holding a child in her arms; she appeared to be in great distress, and as I drew near her, she cried, "Oh, sir, save my child, save my child!" Her husband had died only a few hours before, in a drunken fight, her child was sick and she wished to cross the bridge for help, but for lack of a penny the toll-man would not let her cross. I handed her half a crown and told her she was welcome to that, and more if I had it to spare, but I had but little. The tears were flowing down her cheeks, but not for joy, for her child was just breathing his last. I spread a shawl upon the ground and placed the child on it. It smiled—its earthly troubles were o'er.

Two ladies and a gentleman crossing the bridge at this time, took the mother and her child into their carriage and drove back two miles, where they buried the child, and found a home for the poor woman in a respectable family. She proved very faithful, and she was there when I left the country.

After this I resumed my journey. As I reached the huts a large bell between two upright sticks struck and gave the signal for dinner. I was soon surrounded by about fifty rough specimens of humanity. One asked "Have you any thread, all my buttons are off my breeches." Another, "I want a knife." And as soon as I could hand out my goods, down came the money. The news reached the huts that a peddler was there, and out came women and children in all shapes and clothing; one woman brought a plate of plum pudding, another of roast meat, another a bottle of rum, and urged me to eat and drink. I took the meat and pudding, but the rum I refused, telling them that I preferred cold water. I staid here all night, being treated like a gentleman.

We left Polly and Sally at the Dr.'s house. I will not stop to tell you how they safely arrived at Sally's father's. But before I left Scotland, I made a visit to them. Some rich friend had died and left Polly a nice house and £500. Sally's father had died, but she was married and the mother of two children, namely, Providence and Consolation. When they thought of the degradation from which the Dr. and I had lifted them, they burst into tears, and, throwing their arms around my neck, said, "God bless the day when first you visited the Horse Wind."

Thus ends what I call "my first wanderings."

RETIREMENT.

Solitude seemed pleasanter to me. I was tired of a busy world. I soon became a hermit, and lived over 20 years in different hired hermitages, and under the protection of different Lords and Ladies. I will not in this book mention the different places or individuals.

During this time I played the hermit's part some on the stage; I will mention a fact, which occurred to me then; I fell in with a band of gypsies, who were about to take what little valuables I had with me, and perhaps murder me, but one of their number recognized me, and said, " It is the hermit," and from their superstitious reverence of that class of people gave me no further cause of alarm. Being again without a permanent abode, Lady McDonald, my old friend, of Keppeth Castle offered to make me gardener and give me a home for life, if I would renounce my faith, and become a Catholic.

I do not wish to say anything against the Roman Catholics, for some of my best friends belong to that persuasion; but I told the good lady, that although I thought her a good christian and that she was sincere, I could not change from what I thought my duty. I stayed with her a short time. Soon after I came to America. Lady McDonald has written to me here, and I hold her still as one of my kindest friends.

After my first wanderings, and before I had become a hermit, as I have mentioned, my old landlady died, and I took a notion to remove to Edinburgh, as it was more quiet than Glasgow. My little wanderer was buried here also, and that made the city dearer to me. I took lodgings in the Cannon Gate, this street leads to the royal palace. Although that is nearly in ruins, there are some rooms of state yet

It was in the time of the great Russian war. Her Majesty was then at Balmoral. The great Turkish Sultan had landed with his train of followers, at the Leith roads; her Majesty held a royal banquet at the palace. As I was only a stranger, I was at a loss to know the reason why the street seemed all in a move with carriages. Turning to my landlady, I said, "Nanny, what is to be done at the palace to-night?" She replied, "The Queen is on the throne with the Emperor of the French on her right, the King of Sardinia on her left, while the great Sultan is bending at her feet, asking help to blow up Sebastapol." As the last words fell from her lips, a cold shiver came over me. What a feast for crowned heads.

Across the street lay a poor girl dying of consumption; I had seen her a few days before. She told me all her life, and sore did she grieve at how she had spent it. The sisters of charity had been the means of her conversion; as a brand from the fire, she was saved. As I perceived the room lighted, I said, "Nanny how is that poor girl across the street?" "This night she will be in heaven," she replied, so taking up my hat, I asked her to go with me. As we reached the door of the room where she lay, I heard her say, "Mother, leave me." She was a Lancasterian. They believe it impossible to die if any one is near who loves them. She thought the angels had come to take her spirit home.* So I composed the following lines :—

O, leave me, mother, leave me,
And let the angels come,
*For round my bed they hover,
To waft my spirit home.

In yonder realms above, mother,
My Saviour waiting stands ;
I feel his arms embrace me,
O, leave me in his hands.

Before we left she died. Two of her old companions stood by ; one wept sore, and said, "O, let me catch thy spirit, it will bear me safe through the clouds with you.

As we left the house, I thought there was more joy in heaven over that garret, than all the banquet of the royal palace. She requested me to have a hymn sung as they let the coffin in the grave. She had selected a beautiful one, so I got some S. S. scholars with their teacher to fulfill her wish.

> But at the resurrection morn,
> With lustre brighter far, she'll shine,
> Reviv'd with ever 'during bloom,
> Save from diseases and decline.

MY RICH UNCLE AGAIN.

One day I was looking over a newspaper that had by chance fallen into my hands. My eye fell upon an advertisement inquiring after my grandmother, stating if any of her children were alive, or the next relations, if they were to go to Glenmore, and ask for Mr. Robert Allen, they might hear of something of service to them. It did not make much effect on me, for I thought of the four hours in the stocks, that my old friend Tib and myself had by seeking for riches. My grandmother was dead, and where Tib was I knew not, so I gave it up. But in a few days, Lady McDonald sent me the same information, advising me by all means to go at once; by her letter I found he had removed to another part of the country; so I made up my mind to start on Monday again in search of this rich uncle. As I was in better circumstances this time, I made better speed than on my first journey, and in three days reached the village, near where my rich uncle lived. It was far up in the hills of Bangshire,

As I entered the village, the people came out to gaze after me, for in those days, there were no railroads, and few

strangers to be seen. I entered the "Rest and be Thankful."
I had a little acquaintance with the landlord.

Some of the villagers came in, to inquire if I was going
to give a lecture ; others if I wanted to take a farm ; some
said I was a mountebank and would do wonders on the tight
rope. I assured them that I answered to none of these pur-
poses, but if they would come in the evening, I would sing
a song with the landlord's permission, and show them the
tragedy of the lost child, as I could do it, with the landlord's
assistance ; they thanked me very politely, and said I was a
right sort of a chap for to come among them.

At night the house was full to the door, and good times
we had of it too. I was sorry to leave them, for kinder
hearts I never found ; they could give no information concerning my rich uncle, as he had not been long in the place ;
but they said there was a Mr. Allen, a half crazed man, who
lived five miles up Glenmore. It was an out of the way
place ; and difficult to get at ; so I was very indifferent
about going farther ; but the landlord said, he would send
his boy with me to let me see the place.

A long narrow glen without any road hardly, led us to
my rich uncle's. The people of this glen are the most romantic of any I ever met. When about half way, we came
to a man who had broken down with a load of hay ; there
was a hollow place in the road and it had been filled up with
rough stones, which were likely to break the strongest
teams. I said to the man, " Shall I help you set yourself
right ? " " I wush ye wud mon," he replied. So the lad
and myself put to and got him set a going again. I said "the
road was very bad," and asked if it would not be better for
them to improve them for their own safety ? " Bles ye life
mon, wud I be fule enuf foor to make a road fur others to

make use uf? No, it will do well enuf fur me, I can not be fashed with it." "So you would rather get your teams smashed up, and your horses legs broken before you would make a road for your neighbors?" "They may make the roads as they like fur all me," he said, he "wunna going to be fashed with 'em," and with a crack of the whip across the poor old horse's back, he drove off.

We soon came in sight of my rich uncle's. I gave the boy two shillings and dismissed him, for I thought it best to be alone at the interview.

As I approached the house there seemed to be no person within; I stood at the door and rapped till I was tired, so turning round the corner of the house, I saw a lad busy stuffing his pockets with gooseberries off from the trees; at a distance a lot of pigs were rooting up the potatoes. I called to the boy; he started and set his eyes on me in wild amazement. I said, "My lad, is this Mr. Allen's?" "I guess it is," he replied. "Is he at home?" I asked. "Wy ye I bleve so, who bese ye? ye es baint the doctor? fur ye old one's craze, dunna yo kno?" "And do you call your master crazy? what are you doing, stealing his fruit, and letting the pigs destroy his potatoes?" I said, "Does he pay you wages for that?" Off he was starting, when I asked him to let me see the way to the house. I told him I had stood at the door till I was tired. "Wy, mon, nobuddy gangs to that dure. I mun put these dan pigs out." "I will help you," I said, "and give you sixpence beside, if you will take me to Mr. Allen." Looking at me, he said, "I guess he wud put me down faster'n I went up; and if Polly Stevens should see me off from the sheep she'd pull me lugs, (ears), but if you will give me the sixpence, I will put you to the kitchen door." "But who is this Polly Stevens?" I asked. "Wy, mon, she be the oldoins dorter." "What?" said I, "Is Mr. Allen married?" "I ges he be en, but I never sene his wife.'' "Then it would be better for you to take me right to Polly Stevens," I said. "To Polly Stevens! I ges, she'd put my head into my hands to play with," he said.

As he was taking me through a long shed to the door, he pointed to a large deer, that was skinned and hanging up on a post, and said, " Polly Stevens killed it." "What?" said I, "does Polly go a hunting?" "Wy no, mon, but she alaise takes the gun to plow with her." I started to think what kind of relations I was about to fall in with.

As soon as we reached the door, he left me outside, and running through a narrow passage to the foot of a pair of stairs, he put his finger to his mouth and gave a loud whistle, when a voice answered, "What is it, Tom?" "Wy, cume down Sall, wult ye, here is a mon wonts to see the masther." "What is he like?" asked the female. "I dinna ken, he say he beant the doctor." "I'll be down when I get my hair up." "Cum down whilt, I mun be off to the shepe, before Polly cums," and off he started. In a few minutes down came the maid, who asked me to go into the house; after I had told her who I was, she shewed great respect to me; she said that Mr. Allen had just fallen asleep and to wake him up would make him boisterous; so I said I would wait his sleep. She said she was only the servant; but, "Why does his daughter not prefer to wait upon her father, instead of following the plow?" She replied, "I dare say she is glad to be away from him, for when his fits come on, he is more like the evil one than a man." She said she had been engaged from a distance, but would leave as soon as her time was out.

As soon as the old man woke up, the maid brought me into his presence as a relative. He was very deaf, and it was a long time before she could make him understand who I was. As soon as he heard that I was his sister's son, he tried to get up to meet me, but was not able, so I stepped forward and took his hand. He surveyed me from head to foot; at last he spoke, "Yes, he is my sister's boy, he is." He said he had not been a true brother to my mother, but he "would make it all right with me, he would." He said he was rich, and on conditions "make a gentleman of me, so he would." At this he stopped, and I was looking out of the room window. I saw my fair cousin coming home from plowing, riding one horse and leading the other.

She saw me as she passed to the stable. Like the rest, she also took me for the doctor, therefore she did not make any fuss about seeing me. She opened the door, and paying no attention to me, she went to her father and asked if she should bring his supper up, as she was hungry after a hard day's work. "Why, yes," he said, and pointing to me, continued, "this is your cousin, my sister Nancy's boy." At this she stepped forward and gave me her hand, which I took, and after a few words she got the supper on the table. She asked me if I had taken of any dinner since I came. Her father said we had been so busy talking, he never once thought of that. "But talking does not fill an empty belly," she said. I assured her I was not the least bit hungry.

The old gentleman seemed to think every body was robbing him, even his own daughter.

I stopped a week with my "rich uncle," and no word about the conditions, how I was to become his heir.

At the end of the week, I told him I must return to the city again. He looked at me and said, he was rich, yes he was rich, and if Polly Stevens and I got married, it was ours, but if either one refused, neither of us should get one halfpenny of his money.

He was not going to let it out of his family; he said allthough Polly Stevens was not his own daughter, he had married the mother, and Polly had saved him the expense of keeping a hired man.

So if I chose to marry Polly, he would turn his money over to us at his death; if not I might take my leave without a penny.

I rose up and taking my hat in my hand, I very politely told him, he might give his ill gotten riches to Polly as soon as he pleased, for I could not take her hand, as I had been disappointed already, and had made up my mind to marry no other.

At this he burst out in such a rage, and bade me begone, and never see his face again. I went into the field where Polly was plowing; she stopped her horses, and taking my hand said, "I guess father wants us to get married, but you need not trouble yourself, for I have promised to be Tommy Johnston's wife, and no other man's I'll be; he may give you your portion for my part, and I say its right he should." I told her I liked her the better for her noble resolutions; so we parted. Polly went to plough, whistling as merry as a lark, while I made the best of my way out of the glen.

I reached the tavern again, for to put over the night, for they were among the best hearted people I ever met with. The village people said if I would stop for a month they would pay all expense; but I was anxious to get farther away from my "rich uncle's."

But shortly after he died, and Polly wrote me a letter

that he had, after all, left me the sum of £50. She also asked me to attend the funeral, but I did not get the letter in time, so I did not go. I wrote to her and told her she had more right to the money than I, and wished her to keep it, but this she refused.

In about a year after, she sent me an invitation to her marriage, which I accepted; and Polly makes as good a wife for Tommy Johnston as ever the sun shone on. She handed me the fifty pounds "as a token of friendship between us," she said.

Before I left the country, I went to see her, and she met me with a young Polly, saying the next was to be called Tommy Johnston.

WHY I CAME TO AMERICA.

Many of my visitors ask me the reason why I came to America. If I were the first man to cross the Atlantic, the question might not seem so strange, but with the thousands who come yearly, it seems to me a foolish question. " But " they say, " you are a hermit." " But why," I ask, " should not a hermit have the same right in free America as in other countries ?"

The reasons why I came to America, are simply these :— I gave up the idea of being a hermit any longer, and after spending a few weeks at Lady McDonald's, as I have already mentioned, I took up my abode in a respectable lodging house in Glasgow.

I had not been many hours there, when four men came in and told me that they had taken passage in the " City of Cork" steamer for America, and that there was no place like America since the war. They advised me to join the company and go along with them. The thought came into my mind, that I might drown all my old griefs in the passage, and begin a new life in a strange land. So I went with them and paid my fare to Liverpool, and the next day we were going mountains high upon a stormy ocean.

For days we were fastened down below, to prevent being washed overboard.

I thought of Jonah and the whale's belly, sometimes I fancied that I saw the sharp teeth going to take hold of me. At my side lay a young man from Old Ireland. I shall never forget poor Tom, for that was all of him I ever knew ; but I am sure that poor Tom was ready for death, let it come on sea or land. The door was opened as the storm was supposed to be past its height. I felt inclined to see what was going on upon deck, so getting on an overcoat, I asked Tom if he would go with me, but there he lay, with a hymn book of Wesley's, first singing and then praying. As Tom did not seem inclined to go, I staggered off myself; I reached the deck ; but not to my dying day shall I forget the scene. The ship was heaving up, between two mountains of waves. I fell flat upon my face and the waves went over me. I made the best of my way with a bleeding nose, and a cut upon my head. As I reached the bunk, Tom lay still with his eyes upon the book. I said, "Tom, I think this night we shall see the bottom of the sea, instead of this glorious America." He replied, "I hope we shall land in heaven." I stumbled up into my nest beside Tom, and was going to look what he was so taken up with, for his eyes never left the book, but a side-breaker came, and smash went the windows ; the waters baptized Tom afresh ; a loud scream from the ladies' side told us they were still alive ; out of the bunk I fell and Tom and his book on the top of me ; I got hold of a cross beam, but whether my head or my heels was upmost, I was unable to tell; I felt something holding fast round my waist; so as soon as I could gain a sort of firm footing, I took a look to see what had got so firm a grasp, and to my astonishment, it was a lady. I said, "Madam, if I can render you any assistance I shall be happy to." "My children! my children! where are they?" she exclaimed. "If you can compose yourself and keep hold of this beam," I said, "I will go in search of them." By this time Tom had got himself out of the rabble; tables, barrels of crackers, and a little of everything was rolling up and down the floor. I got the number of the lady's birth and got Tom to try and compose her, while I went in search of the two children; I staggered first to one side of the ship and then the other; at length I found the apartment, but the only occupant was an old Irish woman, who was so busy at her beads, and calling for help from the Virgin, that she paid no attention to me, so I went from one place to another; at length I found the boy. The poor little fellow was nearly trampled to death in a corner. I got him to his mother, and went in search of the little girl. She had been more fortunate, for one of the waiters had taken care of her.

This lady told me she had crossed seven times, but she said she had suffered more during the past hour than through all the voyages. She was rich, and was going to Ohio; she was kind to me, and pressed me to go on with her to her home, "where," she said, "she would repay me," but I thought of Betsey and the country I had left behind.

After reaching New York, I took a notion to see Boston, and I had several letters to deliver to Scotch people in Boston. I came by rail to Springfield. I stopped there a few days and did a little gardening. I took a rather round-about

way, as I wished to see the country. I passed through
Leverett and Locks Pond. As I hove in sight of Wendell, I
beheld three spires, (or what I took for spires, there are but
two), and I called it the city of three churches, for then I
knew not its name, but I have since learned to know and
love the old town. Tom came with me as far as Wendell
depot, but he was a bad traveler, and here he gave up altogether and said, "Bad luck to the ship that brought me over,
there's no place for me like Old Ireland." He was a carpet
weaver and had friends in Philadelphia. He said if he had
the money he'd go to them. I made up what he was lack-
ing his fare; so I took leave of poor Tom, probably never
again to meet in this world. God grant we may in the next
in peace.

The night came on me as I was half way between Orange
and Athol. On the lower side of the road I saw a shed,
into it I crept and scraped what dry rubbish I could get to
make a sort of bed; as I had a good rug which served for my
bed in the ship, I was not so bad off; I soon fell asleep, but
before morning, I thought the shed would be down on the
top of me, for I was woke up by the peals of thunder that
shook the ground. The lightning was truly dreadful. As
soon as the day began to dawn, I set off again. The town
of Athol was all asleep as I passed through; I liked the
appearance of the place, for it looked beautiful in its slumbers. I little thought then, that I should ever become so
well acquainted with its inhabitants, for I truly say the
people of Athol are amongst the noblest who come to the
castle; the sons of Athol appear like gentlemen, her daugh-
ters like ladies. I wish I could say the same for some
nearer home. I next took up my lodging in a vault near
Westminster; the door was open, and being by the way-

side, I never thought of its being a place for the dead till
the next morning as I took the road. At a short distance
stood a building with a padlock on the door outside. What
can be in here! I wondered; seeing a window on the far
side—thinks I, I'll take a peep in; so up I got, but to my
surprise, there stood a hearse clad in plumes of mourning.
A chill came over me, for I had slept all night in some dead
man's grave. The next night I slept at the church horse-
sheds in Briton, and early the next morning I reached
Boston. I went up one street and down another in looking
for lodgings, as the way is, in Old Scotland the people hang
a board out at the window, with "lodgings" on, so that
strangers may apply by seeing the sign; but as I could see
none, I gave it up for a bad job, and was pushing my way
down Richmond street, towards a lot of masts of ships, which
I could see at a distance, for I began to get tired of this way
of tumbling about. So I was thinking as I had still more
money than would pay my fare back again, if there were a
ship ready to sail for old Glasgow, I would bid adieu to
this glorious country, as it had been represented to me. I
did not see much glory in it. I had got half way down Richmond street, when I perceived a sign in a window—"Break-
fasts and dinners at the shortest notice." Why, thinks I,
this is something like home, and as I am hungry, I will peep
inside; so stepping inside, I met a fat woman, not very clean
in her dress. At her ears hung two gold bits, which I saw
were English. I asked for breakfast. She at once took my
hand, and gave me a hearty welcome, for says she—"You
are from Scotland." The tears fell from her eyes, as she
related to me her sorrows; for in Greyfriars' churchyard,
Edinburg, lay her only child; the waves of the Atlantic roll
over her husband, for he died on his voyage.

Her troubled mind seemed to agree well with my own. She got me a good breakfast, and said she had two beds unoccupied, and that I was welcome to one of them if I chose. She was from Belfast, Ireland, but had been a long time in Scotland.

After visiting a few Scotch families, I took a notion to go out into the country, and as the old woman said I could do well by picking blue berries and selling them in Boston, I thought I would start on Monday for the berry fields ; so I took the way out to New Salem, and wandered out to Locks Pond, where I found the rattlesnakes' gutter. There is a cave there also, but it is not so well off for water and fire-wood as this, but the people are much better, and lots of them come over still to see me in this castle. I often regret leaving Leverett and Locks Pond.

As soon as the blueberries were over, the Boston people said I must gather grapes and chestnuts, at last they set me on to make wreaths, for they took a liking for the old Scottie as they called me. It was these wreaths that first brought me to this place, for when I was on the other side of the river gathering blackberries, I used to look at the rocks, and thought some day to take a chance and see them, if no one saw me ; when I began to make wreaths I thought it would be a very good way for to get up into the woods, so I passed through Erving one evening with my blanket on my back, coffee kettle also, as is the way in the old country. As I passed the tavern some low rowdies shouted and hooted after me, but I paid no attention, and passed on. As I came near to the woods, I saw a barn with a house in ruins. Some boys were driving the cows home from a field at the back of the barn. So I passed on as though I would go further, not to let them see me go into the barn, for as the conduct of those I passed in the village was not good, these might be the same.

As soon soon as they were out of sight, I turned back to the barn. It was in pretty good condition then, so I got some hay together into a corner, and spread my blanket and slept well till morning. I then took out my coffee kettle, and made a fire some distance from the barn, near the river side. As I was boiling the coffee, a young lady passed by. She gave a glance at my breakfast fashion and passed on. This lady was what might be called handsome, both in her looks and in her manners, for she had both. When I had got breakfast over, I set off through the woods. It was not an easy job then, for the rubbish was desperate. How I got to this place I never can find out, for on my way I saw curious places that I have never seen since. I left my blanket and coffee pot at a rock near the foot of a wood. When I came to this rock I saw the water coming out of it. "Why," said I, "this is the rock that Moses smote in the wilderness. If ever there was a place for a hermitage, here it is, certainly.

As it was late in the Autumn, I thought it would be better to put the Winter over in Boston, and as I had not made my purse any less, I thought by knitting I should be able to stand the storm, and to come here early next Spring. So as a token of safety, I left a pint tin in the cave ; if the tin was there when I came back, I should stop, if not I would go to Locks Pond again

In the month of March I came back, by the way of Montague this time, not to let the Erving boys know, for I saw from the first time they had not much manners.

The snow was on the ground, but it soon went away. I kept on a good fire, and as there were plenty of trees close

by, it was not very hard. I brought coffee, sugar and a lot
of crackers from Boston, and then set out for Wendell village, where I bought more, for I did not like to go to Erving, as I thought them to be a rough set, by what I saw of
them, and I am very sorry to say that some of them have
proved themselves so to be. Till the blue berries were ripe,
I kept on knitting, and went off to Boston with the stockings,
when I got twelve pair; I always found a ready market for
them.

How much happier was I then than I am now! I often regret to think that' this quiet sort of life should have been
abused. Before I was discovered, I found the cave like a
heaven below, but now it is often the scene of hell. I' do not
object to visitors, but rather encourage them. But to see a
lot come here drunk; others destroy all they can lay their
hands on ; some bring their dogs and all my garden is de-
stoyed with them ; others pull up the flowers and plants by
the roots; and if I tell them not. I only get abuse. Hermitages in other countries are religious institutions ; the great-
est blackguard would not harm a hermit. I often wonder
America should be so void of the sense of hermits. But as
I said before, I do enjoy to see gentlemen and ladies, and
many who come here prove themselves such.

When I was discovered here it was on a Saturday, about
December. The snow had been on the ground for a week
or more. I seldom went out except it was for water or
sticks ; I had got a heap of sticks gathered at some distance
from the cave, and in going out for them had made quite a
track ; a man by the name of Samuel Dirth was out plan-
ning a road for to bring lumber down, and on seeing the
beaten path, could not understand what was going on.

I was busy at the time driving a nail into the old tree

which then stood at the mouth of the cave, for to hang a rug up or to screen the wind from blowing the smoke contrary. I had a stone in my hand, for hammer I had none.

"Hallo!" said a voice outside; I responded, and down went the stone, nail, rug, and I, altogether.

In a minute or so I collected my thoughts, and starting up to my feet, thinks I—It is the landowner or forester; it is as well for me to try and see him, and state how I have intruded upon his land,—but not a sign of a man appeared to enter. I stepped out, but to my great astonishment the man was going as fast as his legs could carry him. What to do I was at a loss to know; I sat stupid. To go to Boston would take all the money I had to put over the winter, and I had bought nearly enough flour and meal to last the storm.

To carry it back to the rattlesnake gutter was one thought.

As I was a stranger in this country, I was at a loss what to do; for in Scotland it is a serious crime to be trespassing in the woods, owing to the game laws.

But the day went by and no sign of a man appeared; Sunday passed in the same way.

I began to think it must be a ghost, for I had come across a heap of bones a few days before, but after a full survey of them I concluded they must have been beast's bones.

On Monday morning I got up, thinking it must have been a man gathering chestnuts, or something like myself.— So taking up my knitting, I set to work again and sang as I worked, some of my favorite tunes, "Balerma," "Old Hundred," "Jerusalem," "Comfort," "Rockingham," and the like.

I had not sat long before I heard some one talking, so getting up, at a distance I saw three men approaching;

one had an ax, another a spade, the third a pick. What, can these be the constables, thought I? What rough weapons they must carry in this country.

At last one ventured to approach a little nearer, he stood in the door of the cave, till I bid him come in.

After a few words I found him to be a very sociable young fellow, he asked the other two to come also, and after a little explanation on my part. they seemed satisfied and went to work.

The man Samuel Dirth, has always been like a father to me, and told me I might make a home on his grounds if any thing occurred to remove me from here.

The other two are still among my best friends.

The news reached the village and soon some ladies found the way up; rough as it was, it did not frighten them. I many times think the women of America are a much braver cast than the men; at least I like them much better.

Sunday came and the place was crowded; some of the best young men brought a board each; others brought provisions; these were not the rich people of Erving, but those who worked for their daily bread. Some of them put up the boards for to screen the wind; but they were not long before some of the baser sort, when I was absent, destroyed all they could lay their hands on; twice have they pulled down the place; they have stopped up the road; one even stood and demanded pay from visitors. The selectmen have done nothing to prevent it. Some have spread false reports to other places about the " Old Hermit."

They have put taxes on me, which I pay each year. Some suppose I have received remuneration for damages—as I should—but this is not so.

But why go on—though I might write more—and every

word be true—this is in the past—and as I wish the Almighty and ever blessed Father, through his only Son, my Redeemer to forgive me—so by the help of that blessed Saviour, I will try to forgive.

I will add that amongst those who have most abused me, are some who having become better acquainted with me, have used me very kindly, and behave here like gentlemen—and I often repeat the prayer of a certain lady who on this very rock in a prayer meeting, earnestly asked the Giver of all good to abundantly pour out his spirit on this town, that every heart might be touched. She prayed earnestly—and with strong faith—and she said if we had but faith as a grain of mustard seed, every soul in Erving would be converted; she prayed that this rock might become the temple of the living God. May the Great Jehovah answer this.

SABBATH MORNING.

Again the day of rest returns with balmy incense from its Lord; another week of our pilgrimage is o'er; what silence reigns within these rocks—as if the majesty of heaven was going to descend as upon Sinai's height; the spot is grand and beautiful; 'tis an everlasting feast to look on the beauties of nature and exclaim—"The earth is the Lord's and the fulness thereof;—and who shall set the bounds of his habitation." But this quietness will soon be broken—for at a distance I hear the noise of some intruders. What a pity the house of God could not draw them to the fountain of living waters; instead of coming to drink where they are not satisfied.

LOCATION.

The Castle is situated in the midst of a forest of some 400 acres, about a mile and a half northwest of Erving center; those stopping at the depot can obtain conveyance from the hotel, which is kept by the accommodating and hospitable F. S. Hagar,—meals can be obtained there and also at the foot of the hill, where cars will stop if passengers wish to visit the hermitage.

The cave itself is situated at the foot of an immense wall of granite, facing the south, which rises by broken steps as it recedes, until it terminates in a mountain of rock, reminding one of the couplet,

> " Hills peep o'er hills,
> And Alps on Alps arise."

The scenery is grand, majestic—the sublimity of these works not only reminds me of the romantic Highlands of my native Scotland, but my own spirit is in harmony with these deep solitudes. Indeed I think no lord in his castle or king in his palace happier than I.

The former owners of the land, Messrs. Burt & Wright, of Springfield, made me a visit soon after I was first discovered. They expressed much interest in me, and kindly assured me that I might live here as long as I chose. (The land is now owned by Mr. Samuel Holmes of Erving, who is a good friend to me.)

I now felt that the prayer so often offered, that I might be allowed to remain in this cave was answered, and my heart was filled anew with praise and thankgiving. It seemed to me then, and does so still, that a kind Providence directed me to America, and provided for me this home, and I cannot but cherish the hope that here I may be allowed to spend the remainder of my days.

MY PETS.

My rabbit, who held claim here before I came, cheered me in my loneliness, and became quite tame. My mouse, Frisky, so named on account of his liveliness, had become so tame as to eat bread from my hand, and would march around the cave, turning summersaults and amusing the visitors with his gymnastics.

Two birds soon built their nests in the cave, and a family of sqirrels became very neighborly, but these are all gone now, and my only pets are my two cats, Laddie and Pacan and their two children, Rodney (Hunt) and Tinker.

SIZE OF THE CAVE.

I have enlarged the cave not by the work of a chissel, but by the heating of a rock and dashing on cold water, so that the presnt size is about twenty feet square,—the height at the largest, is about eight feet, then sloping back to the ground.

A friend of mine while visiting here one day took down some paper and, as he said, scribbled a few lines to a friend. I begged him for a part of it, which I here inclose, as it gives a sketch of each place of interest.

> But now of the hermitage let us talk,
> Of Dexter Street and Princess Walk,
>   Of Sorrowsvale—the Sisters' Seat,
>   Named for two mourning sisters sweet.
> For those who send flowers, a street he will name,
> And the flowers are planted on the same.
>   A southern slope, Stafford Street is named
>   For a certain family quite famed.

Tower Street leads from this to the Castle,
A dangerous place for young men to wrestle.
  Northfield Center and Phillipston Heights,
  Rattlesnakes' Den, where the ladies have useless frights.
The Promenade and Main Street, too,
From which is obtained a most excellent view.
  Athol Depot the Summer Seat,
  Is connected to Main by Athol Street.
Orange Street leads to the Castle from Main,
And Montague Road goes on to the Plain.
  A grand look-out is obtained from the Tower—
  A beautiful place is Eden Bower.
Pulpit Rock (there is sometimes preaching there,)
Is just outside the Castle which is twenty teet square.
  The rock roof of the Castle all varnished with smoke,
  Causes much admiration from visiting folk.
By the fire side is the Hermit's bed,
The reception room is a wooden shed.
  And many a lord and lady fair,
  Have come to see the Hermit there.
The Castle is of such renown,
That orders come from London Town,
  From North, from South, from East, from West,
  For songs and pictures of the Hermit's rest.
At Moses' Rock let's take a look,
From which flows out the Laddie's brook.
  The Cat Castle is just beyond,
  With caves and crevices hard to count,
And Laddie here enjoys his life,
In peace and harmony with " Pacan his wife."

LITTLE TOBY'S GRAVE.

The following lines were written by the Hermit of Erving Castle, (Erving, Mass.) in memory of a favorite Cat, Toby, which was killed in March, 1870. They are printed at the suggestion of his numerous lady friends.

Rest, little Toby, rest—
　　Not in the Hermit's cave,
But underneath the sods so green,
　　Is little Toby's grave.

Rest, little Toby, rest—
　　Sleep in thy peaceful grave.
The wretch that took thy life away
　　Is but the devil's slave.

The flowers bloom around you,
　　Although you see them not—
Your resting place is sacred,
　　Your mem'ry not forgot.

I hear a rush down the garden walk,
　　The ladies are gone there
To leave a laurel at his head,
　　　I can see his grave from here.

Who will watch my dying gasp,
　　Or who will mourn for me,
Since little Toby's breathed his last,
　　And died upon my knee?

I, too, must take a last farewell,
　　My little pet, my pride;
But who will mourn the Hermit's death
　　Since little Toby's died.

The days to years roll on,
　　The season comes and goes;
Thy grave reminds me of my own,
　　When God his time shall chose.

THE HERMIT OF ERVING CASTLE.

BY MRS. MARIA L. BURNETTE.

Up among the jagged rocks and cliffs,
   Just west of Erving town,
There is a noted spot, the Hermit's Cave,
   A place of great renown.

From far and near they come,
   The high, the low, the rich and gay,
To see this strange and curious man,
   And unto him their homage pay.

Then let us mingle with the crowd
   That daily gathers at his door,
And learn the reason, if we can,
   Why he calls this world a bore.

Why he shuns the haunts of men,
   And leads a hermits life,
Never sighs for the innocent prattle of a child,
   Or the gentle ministrations of a wife.

As you reach his door,
   He greets you with a happy face,
And kindly takes you by the hand,
   And bids you welcome to his fairy place.

I can't describe this man to you,
   So wont attempt the task to-day;
But you can see yourself sorrows
   He has had, though he seems so gay.

I asked him why he shunned the world,
   And never mingled with the throng;
With trembling voice he answered me,
   A woman's hand hath done the wrong.

It was the same *old*, *old* story,
　Acted over and over again ;
How a woman led him on to love,
　Then crushed his heart with grief and pain.

How he built up airy castles,
　In his heart a woman did enthrone ;
How she heartless left him
　To wander in this world alone.

And to forget his sorrows
　He left his native home,
And seeks among our quiet hills
　A Hermit's life alone.

Now, friends, if you wish to pass a day,
　And dull time would kill,
You'll find no better way than to visit
　John, the Hermit, in his Castle on the hill.

Erving, July 23, 1871.

SMILING MAY.

BY THE HERMIT OF ERVING CASTLE.

Like an angel's form she left me,
　So spotless, so divine ;
But her heart it was another's—
　It never could be mine.
But few have loved as I have lov'd,
　A love that lasts for aye ;
And in this breast still lingers
　A love for Smiling May.

Like an angel's form she left me,
  With the love light in her eye ;
Her auburn hair in braids so neat
  Might all this world defy.
But that hair was braided not for me,
  That eye is turn'd away,
While this poor heart is breaking
  For the love of Smiling May.

With her I've watched the moon so bright,
  For her I crossed the flood ;
With her I broke the ring in two—
  And wrote the lines in blood.
I see her in my slumbers ;
  I hear her steps by day ;
And in this heart still lingers
  A love for Smiling May.

My summer's sun will soon go down,
  And like the winter's blast,
Then sorrow will have done its work,—
  The heavy conflict's past.
When in the dust this head is laid,
  Then all the world may say—
    Here lies a heart that liv'd and died
  For none but Smiling May.

Extract from the Athol " Worcester West Chronicle."

JOHN THE HERMIT.—It is inscribed in Holy Writ that it is not good for man to be alone. Although this fact is an out-breathing of Deity, yet many of human kind have at various times and places, and from all kinds of religious, moral and pecuniary reasons, tried hard to gainsay it, and by their actual life endeavored to demonstrate the many charms of solitude that lie hidden in cloister and hermitage.

For instance, we have among the craggy cliffs of our neighboring town of Erving, a hermit who fain would establish among our granite rocks and limpid streams a fac-simile of the hermitages of Albion and Scotia.

Among the domains of England's nobility, it is customary to have a romantic spot inhabited by a hermit, with long disheveled hair, matted beard, and finger-nails like the talons of an eagle, who daily adds additional charms to render the surroudings more and more picturesque. This is the desire of our John, and explains our statement of his being a hermit by profession. * * * *

He is without doubt, very industrious in his mountain home, as his garden and the many improvements in and about the place will well show.

He is largely visited from all the neighboring towns.

The scenery from the crags around is indeed romantic, and will in itself repay a visit. We would say to our readers, go and see Erving Castle.

.

www.ingramcontent.com/pod-product-compliance
Lightning Source LLC
Chambersburg PA
CBHW022032080426
42733CB00007B/809